Square Butte, southwest of Great Falls

Photograph of Charles M. Russell, Courtesy C.M. Russell Museum,
Great Falls, Montana

Published by Thomasson-Grant, Inc., Frank L. Thomasson III and John F. Grant, Directors
Designed by Megan R. Youngquist and Marilyn F. Appleby
Edited by Carolyn M. Clark
Photographs copyright © 1987 Sam Abell. All rights reserved.
Introduction copyright © 1987 Ginger Renner. All rights reserved.
Excerpts from GOOD MEDICINE by Charles M. Russell. Copyright 1929, 1930 by Nancy C. Russell.
Reprinted by permission of Doubleday & Company, Inc.
This book, or any portions thereof, may not be reproduced in any form
without written permission of the publisher, Thomasson-Grant, Inc.
Photography may not be reproduced without permission of Sam Abell.
Introduction may not be reproduced without permission of Ginger Renner.
Library of Congress catalog number 86-050718
ISBN 0-934738-21-1
Printed and bound in Japan by Dai Nippon Printing Co., Ltd.
Any inquiries should be directed to the publisher, Thomasson-Grant, Inc.,
505 Faulconer Drive, Suite 1C, Charlottesville, Virginia 22901, telephone (804) 977-1780.

THOMASSON-GRANT

CM Russell's
WEST

With compliments of
Earle M. Chiles
Best wishes!

Sam Abell
May 1987.

PHOTOGRAPHY BY SAM ABELL
INTRODUCTION BY GINGER RENNER

WHEN I WAS A KID, 1905

watercolor and gouache, 14″ × 11″

Courtesy Frederic G. Renner

MONTANA, like "all Gaul," is divided in three parts. The Eastern section rolls into the Dakota flatlands in ever-diminishing waves, the land scored by the valleys of two great rivers, the Missouri and the Yellowstone. It is marked by seemingly unceasing winds which try the patience of men and women alike, tease and pluck at the topsoils of the region, determine the shapes and growth of shrubs and trees, and batter the ubiquitous prickly pear whose capabilities for survival increase under the adverse vagaries of Montana's climate. All living things that thrive—or even just exist—under Montana's demanding weather are the tougher for the experience.

Along certain areas of the escarpments that border the twisting course of the Missouri River the wind has acted as a giant sculptor, carving out extensive stretches of battlements and turrets reminiscent of castles on the Rhine. In other areas the facades suggest the lines of sorrowful saints which guard the doors of Gothic cathedrals.

It is a strange, often empty, land worn by extremes of temperature, lying under an endless vault of sky.

The middle area differs from the Eastern sector. It is higher, of course, as the land rises toward its destiny. Its valleys are fertile, and with more rainfall its grasses are taller, the earth-hugging buffalo grass of the Eastern plains replaced by bluestems, wheatgrasses, and fescues. In the mid-1880s, these tough, nutritious grasses were endangered by the tremendous herds of both sheep and cattle thrown into this vast grazing ground or, in later years, by immigrant farmers who, not recognizing the limitations of this land, plowed it under. Slowly, by more thoughtful and caring range practices these grasses have been re-established, but there are few places where they grow stirrup-high as they did when the white man first came into the area.

The area is distinguished by lonely clumps of high mountains with intriguing names—the Belts, the Snowys, the Crazies, the Highwoods. Left over eons back by violent upheavals, now they are smoothed down, gentled, heavily forested, and isolated.

To the West the land rises abruptly. Charlie Russell once described it as "the big hills... where the teeth of the world tear holes in the clouds." These soaring peaks have been both fortresses and barriers. They enclosed areas of isolated safety for early Indian tribes: Shoshoni, Piegan, and Flathead. They were, at the same time, a formidable wall breached with great difficulty by the Lewis and Clark party and subsequent travelers through this awesomely beautiful land. The valleys these mountains enclosed were rich in soil and water, and many of them in Montana were rich in the earth's elusive treasures.

When the sun rises hesitantly over the Eastern edge of Montana, it streaks the sky with thin shafts of red-orange light. Sometimes, when high clouds move with elegiac grace toward that

Bison skull and cement scratchings, Russell's Bull Head Lodge,
Glacier National Park

rising sun, the horizon is marked by odd, parallel lines of color—crimson next to the prairie's edge, often an added layer of washed-out green, a pale and acid green fading into bleached blue, which in turn is absorbed by the fading indigo of a five-in-the-morning sky.

At the same time the sun is chasing the blue-violet of night from the coulees and gullies of Eastern Montana, it is washing the tops of the Western mountains with an orange-pink glow. The lands in between, the vast stretches of rolling prairies, broad valleys, and shining mountains, are revealed by long shafts of horizontal light.

In latter days, Montana has been known by two descriptions, Big Sky Country and The Treasure State. The one extols the grandeur above, the other, beneath this great earth. One name comes from the astounding stretches of ever-varying skies, towering with shining, white-edged thunderheads, determining the land, bringing the rain, or holding it back. The other designation brings to mind what first called so many men to this great region: the gold, silver, copper, coal, and yes, the bright sapphires dug from the heart of the land.

It was not the land itself, the beauty above, or the treasure below that called young Charles Marion Russell from the security of a well-established St. Louis home. It was the persistant dream of a way of life he came seeking—a way of life which, in reality, no longer existed when Charlie arrived in 1880. What Charlie found was a home, and while he never pursued the treasures in the earth, he came to love the land passionately. Although the way of life he sought was a romantic dream, by his unwavering vision he has preserved aspects of that life to the present day.

In that fateful spring when 16-year-old Charlie Russell first arrived in Montana Territory, he came with the desire and for the express purpose of "being a cowboy."

Not a *real cowboy*, you understand. A real cowboy worked seven days a week, twelve to 15-hour days, and, occasionally, around the clock. A real cowboy slept on the ground under open skies for weeks on end, in drizzle, driving rain, or the misery of a snowstorm, and sometimes during bitterly cold nights shared his bed gear with another cowboy for the comfort provided by body heat. He accepted without a murmur the almost military discipline of a cattle drive or roundup, and endured being summarily dismissed at the end of the drive with no such security as unemployment insurance. He worked under these conditions for the princely sum of a dollar a day and keep—usually providing his own saddle and bed gear and often throwing one or more of his own horses into the remuda. He suffered cuts and abrasions and rope-burned hands with no complaints. With sprained ankles or torn ligaments wrapped in old cloths soaked in witch hazel and alcohol by the cook, he got back on his horse with not so much as an encouraging shoulder-pat from a fellow rider. A real cowboy considered his job the best in the world, and thought of himself as free and independent, yet never questioned and seldom defied the authority and direction of the Captain or foreman of the roundup. And above all, he knew full well that on a scale from 1-to-10, the cow herd rated "10," while he, the cowpuncher, came in about a "3."

CMR hat, boots, and sash, Great Falls

CMR studio with SMOKE SIGNAL on the easel, Great Falls

No, it was not to be a real cowboy that Kid Russell came West. Rather, it was to be part of a romantic dream, to relive a kind of life that had passed into history a quarter of a century earlier.

No one knows just how far back in Charlie's life this particular dream began. Perhaps it was genetically transferred. It seems that from the very earliest age the boy was completely absorbed by visions of the West. The exploits and adventures of his great uncles, the Bent brothers, told and retold at family gatherings at Charlie's grandmother's home, affected the young boy profoundly. All of the adventurous, hardy, self-reliant, colorful, idiosyncratic characters who were associated with Charles and William Bent, the Kit Carson-Jim Beckwourth-Uncle Dick Wooten bunch, simply magnified young Charlie's dream. Apparently he never recognized, or certainly did not dwell upon, the tragedies that marked their lives. What Charlie thought of, what he dreamed about, what he wanted to emulate was the independence, freedom, exploits, and exciting ventures that he perceived through the retelling of their life stories.

Although the Bent brothers were moldering in lonely Western graves long before Charles Marion Russell was born, their lives reached out across the years to this romantic boy, and his fate was sealed by their influence.

Oddly, though he had not intended it, Charlie did live the life of a real cowboy, at least for the better part of eleven years (give or take a year or so, depending upon how much faith one has in the veracity of the various characters in this not-so-small drama). Charlie himself was not given to placing great emphasis on specific years or dates when it came to that early period in Montana.

Oh! he never pretended to be a "top hand," one who could tame or gentle a bronc, rope mulish, mean-minded longhorn cows, or who, just for sport, would team up with another top hand to rope a grizzly bear. He signed on first as a night wrangler watching over, riding slowly around, the gently drifting horse herd. It was said he "held 'em purty close," but hold them, he did. And he graduated to night herding the cattle, mesmerizing, soothing the milling bunch with off-key, low-sung chants. Cows, after all, are not known for tone sensitivity, but they like the reassurance that security is close by.

It was a job demanding a sense of responsibility, a considerable degree of reliability, and a young fellow who could get by with four-and-a-half hours of sleep daily, plus some dozing time. Charlie did it with pride. Years later, he wrote, "I was neither a good roper nor rider. I was a night wrangler. How good I was, I'll leave it for the people I worked for to say—there are still a few of them living. In the spring I wrangled horses, in the fall I herded beef. I worked for the big outfits and always held my job."

It was a dream life that Charles Russell came to embrace in Montana Territory, one he was prepared to defend to the end of his days. Granted, he caught the apogee of expansion—and unfortunately of dissolution—of the open-range cattle industry. Nothing before or after ever matched the excitement of the years 1880 to 1887 in Montana.

CMR home and log cabin studio, Great Falls
Jack Russell in the bedroom where his father died, Great Falls

Fred Renner, CMR expert, holding
MEXICAN BUFFALO HUNTERS

Later, Charlie, doing a better job than anyone else, wrote the epitaph on that remarkable period:

I spent New Years in Lewistown   you wouldnt know the town or the country either   its all grass side down now   where once you rod circle and I night rangled a gopher couldnt graze now   the boosters say its a better country than it ever was but it looks like hell to me   I liked it better when it belonged to God   it was shure his country when we knew it

Charlie saw himself and his life in terms of this personal dream which he so passionately wished to make real. Almost from the beginning of his life in Montana he was lamenting the changes taking place. In his view there was a holy quality about this wide-open, untouched land when he first knew it. Time and again he made such references to when the land "belonged to God."

Charlie did not ascribe to either his cowpuncher associates or the cattlemen who owned the big herds any responsibility for the changes he deplored. The cattlemen were, after all, "regular men;" they shared Charlie's views. The open land, the free land, the unfenced land was the way it had been for all time, and that, in his opinion, was how it should remain. The huge herds competing for grass and water had no part in the land's devastation. Only the farmer, the "punkin roller," or the homesteader, "the nester," who put up barbed wire and plowed under native grasses, only they were the culprits. Russell wrote:

I came west 31 years ago   at that time baring the Indians and a fiew scatered whites the country belonged to God   but now the real estate man and nester have got moste of it grass side down and most of the cows that are left feed on shugar beet pulp   but thank God I was here first...

To his friend Grovent in the spring of 1920, Charlie wrote:

You are right   we are not young   But we lived when meat was plenty and we didn't have to hide when we drank or gambled   one day then was worth more than 20 years of living now   We got the cream   these late comers are getting skim milk   Grovent we got no kick coming.

And all the time he grieves for the loss of "free grass and no fences," he reinforces his vision. He will make the dream come true—if only on paper or canvas. He paints another compelling, if reconstructed, scene. And we have *Free Trappers, Pay Dirt,* or *Romance Makers* to reinforce our own present-day fantasies.

Charlie may have grieved over the changes he saw around him, but this did not diminish his fervent devotion and commitment to the lands of Montana and beyond. Russell enjoyed new sights and places, and wherever he and his wife Nancy traveled, he was remarkably astute in gathering bits of local history and folklore. He used innumerable backgrounds and settings for his paintings: the live oaks and coastal mountains of Southern California, the misty seaside of the Northwest, the long, low mesas of Arizona, the high plains of Alberta, the deep woods of England, the streets of Cairo, the beaches of Florida, and the cactus-clad hills of Chihuahua.

But nothing anywhere could compete with home. One really gets to know the land from the back of a horse, and he had ridden on horseback over much of Montana's hills and valleys, coulees and canyons. Montana sustained him; it fulfilled and comforted him. When he was far from home, he readily admitted he was lonely: "California is alright but I cant see Belt or Square Butte from here   Frank give my best wishes to Montana   nobody's bared," and, "Friend Trigg as I am lonsum to night and far from my range I thought it might help some to write you   Just think I am in a camp of four million and I guess I know about eight   it makes me feel small."

One aspect of Charlie Russell's personality, well established when he first came to Montana Territory, was a fascination with the native tribes of the country. This attitude was not shared by many Montanans; only four years had passed since the battle at Little Big Horn. Memories were still fresh of that debacle, and trust was not a common characteristic of the relations between the red and the white man. Montana newspapers reported regularly on the movements of small bands of Indians, as though to warn their subscribers to beware.

As a boy, Russell filled sketch books with pictures of Indians, identifying them as coming from different tribes although his Ute, Kiowa, and Commanche Indians were all dressed the same and looked to be brothers. But Charlie drew these Indians both in casual, everyday situations and as menacing, terror-inspiring characters.

Years later, Charlie admitted to moments of uneasiness when he first met Indians on his initial trip into the Judith Basin. And he made a great story out of an encounter with two Indian men at Jake Hoover's camp; the boy is alone, the Indians demand food, and Charlie cooks pancakes faster than he has ever done anything in his life—just to fill them up and get them out!

At some time in those first years in Montana, the wariness in the boy ceased. It very likely occurred while he lived with Jake Hoover, the entrepreneurial mountain man who was Charlie's first friend and mentor in Big Sky Country. Jake, big in size and heart, was a friend to the Indians. They came to trust him and knew they could always count on a handout at Jake's camp. Jake's attitude toward the Indians reassured the boy, and he sought out the small bands of nomads, drawn by their strange and colorful clothing, attracted to their unemcumbered lifestyle.

As a young man, he became the friend of the Indians, learning their sign language, accepting their social patterns, respecting their religious beliefs. Above all, he admired their relationship with and their attitude toward the land. Much of the dominate philosophy of Russell's mature years reveals its origin in an Indian way of life.

The Duwamish Chief Seattle, a great friend of the white settlers in the Northwestern corner of this country, was much admired by Charles Russell, so much so that the artist painted a strikingly handsome study of the noted Indian leader standing in the prow of his carved and painted canoe in the running seas of Puget Sound. Among many bits of wisdom passed on by Seattle was the following:

Bill Trask at the Jake Hoover cabin he restored, Little Belt Mountains
CMR grave, Highland Cemetary

This we know: earth does not belong to man: man belongs to the earth. This we know. All things are connected. Whatever befalls the earth befalls the sons of the earth. Man did not weave the web of life: he is merely a strand in it. Whatever he does to the web he does to himself.

Russell subscribed to this philosophy completely. But it was only one of many things that bulwarked his admiration and respect for the Indians. To a friend, he wrote: "Ive known some bad Injuns but for every bad 'un I can match 'im with ten white   man for man an Injun's as good as a white man any day   No Injun ever did me dirt and many a ones done me favors   When he's good friend he's the best friend in the world." And to Senator Paris Gibson, Russell wrote: "The Injun was a war lover but blamed no God for the blood he split   Neither for cross nor King did he war but for his country   and well we know it was worth fighting for   a damn good country and a damn good cause."

If Charles Russell single-mindedly viewed his own life in a wishful rather than in a realistic manner, in the same way he assuaged his problems with the Indians of the Northern Plains. He had had a dream vision of the Indians' lives and ways since boyhood. By the time Charlie got to Montana, most Indians had been relegated to reservations. It is quite possible that Russell saw the vestiges of a buffalo hunt when a small band of Blackfeet came into the Judith Basin, desperate to augment the meager government handout that was now their principal source of food. The Indian was rapidly being stripped of his freedom, his dignity, his way of life. This was simply unacceptable to Charlie. Since he could not stop this tidal wave of change, he did the next best thing. He recreated—first in his mind and then through his art—the Indians as they *had* been.

During his lifetime, Russell produced probably 2,500 pieces of art depicting Indians. Of that remarkable body of work, no more than a handful portrayed the Indian as he truly was when Charlie came to Montana Territory seeking his dream. Charlie's Indians ride forever over endless stretches on fine horses wearing handsome and exotic accouterments. They clash in a crescendo of sound and action with life-long enemies; they take their ease in the shadow of their tipis in camps filled with food and the sweet, gentle activities of home; they return, victorious and safe, from successful horse-stealing raids. They walk or ride, tall and proud, filled with dignity.

The body of art work Charlie Russell left behind set the standards, provided inspiration for succeeding generations of painters and sculptors. But that's Art—a creation of the imagination and of the heart.

Perhaps he just might also have inspired a generation or two of buckeroos. They are still around the West, riding in all sorts of weather, although sometimes, now, in pickup trucks, doing all the jobs necessary to keep cows in good shape, branding and cropping ears and giving shots—and still thinking that they are independent and totally free.

Ginger Renner

Claude Saylor and two hands, Fort Peck Lake, Charles M. Russell Wildlife Refuge

THE REAL OUTDOORS

WHEN THE LAND BELONGED TO GOD, 1914

oil, 42½″ × 72″

Courtesy Montana Historical Society, Museum Purchase

...the camp you live in now can bost of man made things but your old hom is still the real out doors and when it coms to making the beautiful ma nature has man beat all ways from the ace and that old lady still owns a lot of montana...

CMR

Pronghorn male, National Bison Range, Mission Mountains

National Bison Range, Moiese

…the Rocky mountians would have been hard to reach with out him

he fed the explorer   the great fur trade wagon tranes felt safe when they reached his range

he fed the men that layed the first ties across this great west   Thair is no day set aside where he is an emblem

the nickle weares his picture dam small money for so much meat   he was one of natures bigest gift and this country owes him thanks…

CMR

Three deer in velvet, the "high country," Dana Ranch

WHITE TAILS, 1896
watercolor, 12″ × 18¼″
Courtesy of Mongerson Wunderlich Galleries,
Chicago, Illinois

Above the breaks, Missouri River

Citadel Rock, Missouri River

...if its laying down you need Lake McDonald is the best bed ground in the world and my lodge is open and the pipe lit for you and yors   you know that Lake country sings the cradle song to all who lay in her lap...

CMR

Lake McDonald from Russell's Bull Head Lodge, Rocky Mountains, Glacier National Park

PLAINS INDIANS

THE MEDICINE MAN, 1908
oil, 29¾" × 48"
Courtesy Amon Carter Museum, Fort Worth

The Red man was the true American   They have almost gon but will never be forgotten   The history of how they faught for their country is written in blood a stain that time cannot grinde out   their God was the sun   their Church all out doors   their only book was nature and they knew all its pages

CMR

Blood Indian sun dance, Standoff, Alberta

(Above and opposite) Tepee of Pete Standing Alone, Standoff

Pete Standing Alone holding War Bonnet Woman

Medicine bundle of Pete Standing Alone

Blood Indian Kainai Ceremony, Standoff

Dancers at the Crow Fair, Crow Reservation

Blood Indian dancers, Standoff

Rufus Goodstriker, a Blood Indian medicine man

PIEGAN CHIEF, 1912

watercolor, 14″ × 12″

Courtesy Rockwell Museum, Corning, New York

Crow Indians watering horses, Little Big Horn River

...the Indian is a great student of nature and knowes her well   it takes a thief to catch a thief   it also takes an Indian to fool an Indian. he knows that some far off butte holds a sentinal who is as motionless as the rocks about him but his beed eyes see all for miles not a s[p]eck on the planes escape his keen sight   he will read the puffs of a signal smoke miles away as his whit cousin would a book   if a distant heard is suddenly disturbed while grazing he studies out the cause   if the wild goos circles his feeding ground an failes to light it is man that has caused it   nature is his mother and she talks with her child...

CMR

Rana Realbird wearing an elk's tooth dress, Wyola

Dancer at the North American Indian Days, Blackfeet Indian Reservation, Browning

Parade of dancers, Browning

REGULAR MEN

THE ROUNDUP #2, 1913

oil, 25″ × 49″

Courtesy Montana Historical Society, Mackay Collection

...I am still in Montana and still working on the range   we are at present bissy gathering horses for the spring youndup   the cattel have all been driven north to milk rive [Milk River] and I leave for their in a fiew days   it is a pritty good cow Country   the fellow that told you I was sketching for a Magizane was misstaken as I have been on the range all the time   I have tirde several times to make a living painting but could not make it stick and had to go back to the range   I expect I will have to ride till the end of my days but I would rather be a poor cow puncher than a poor artist...

CMR

Lyle Chamberlain shooting a dry cow, near the Mussellshell River

Newborn calf, Leroy Strand Ranch, Square Butte

Fall roundup, Krone Ranch, Haystack Butte

Longhorn cow and calf, Mike Bryant Ranch, Square Butte

50

...I have made a living painting pictures of the horned on and the life about him   it took regular men to handle real cows...God made cows with hornes to defend herself and when a wolf got meat it wasent easy   often he was so full of horn holes he wasent hungry...

CMR

XO brand of Wertheimer Ranch, part of the old OH Ranch where CMR was a night herdsman, Utica

Branding and castration, Ken Rosman Ranch, Buffalo

Bryant Mikkelson, Ken Rosman Ranch, Buffalo

Bob Bovee, Hook Ranch, Custer County

Floyd Forbes whistling to round up the cattle, Wertheimer Ranch, Utica

56

Two cowboys rounding free-roaming horses, Joe Vassau's Flying X Ranch, Forsythe

… as I said before use paint but dont get smeary let sombody elce do that keep on making real men horses and cows of corse the real artistick may never know you but nature loving regular men will and thair is more of the last kind in this old world an thair the kind you want to shake hands with…

CMR

Claude Saylor in his branding wagon, Brusett

UNDER THE SKY

WILD HORSE HUNTERS, 1913
oil, 30⅛" × 47"
Courtesy Amon Carter Museum, Fort Worth

...I was out on a buffalo roundup in October I wish youd been along it was on the Flat Head reservation, an open, wild country we saw lots of wild hosses never getting closer than a mile an dont ever think they wasent wild it seemeded like they all ways winded us before we sighted them   they were all ways running...

CMR

Riding out after the horses, Flying X Ranch

Matt Urick, Belt

Taking the horses to line camp, Flying X Ranch

(Above and opposite) Pony roundup for branding and inoculation

Joe Vassau, Jr.

Arnold Vassau

Line camp at noon

...I think it was about this time of year thirty sevon years ago that we first met at Babcocks ranch in Pigeye bason on the upper Judith   I was living at that time with a hunter and trapper Jake Hoover who you will remember   He and I had come down from the south fork with three pack horses loaded with deer and elk meet which he sold to the ranchers and we had stopped for the night with old Bab, a man as rough as the mountians he loved but who was all hart from his belt up and friends ore strangers were welcom to shove there feet under his table   this all welcom way of his made the camp a hangout for many homeless mountian and prairie men and his log walls and dirt roof semed like a palice to those who lived mostly under the sky

the eavning you came there was a mixture of bull whackers hunters and prospecters who welcomed you with hand shaks and rough but friendyl greetings

I was the only stranger to you so after Bab interduced Kid Russell he took me to one side and whispered

boy says he I don't savy maney samsingers but Brother Van deels square...

CMR

Frank Urick, Belt

Centennial, colt born on the wagon train from Jordan to Miles City,
named for the Montana Stockgrowers Centennial

...A lady with manicured fingers can drive an automobile with out maring her polished nailes   But to sit behind six range bred horses with both hands full of ribbons   these are God made animals and have branes. To drive these over a mountain rode takes both hands feet and head an its no ladys job...

CMR

Choteau County wagon train, Little Belt Mountains

Jordan spoke of the Miles City wagon train, coming out of the Badlands

Buffalo roundup, National Bison Range, Moiese

PABLO-ALLARD BUFFALO DRIVE, 1909
watercolor, 9″ × 12″
Courtesy Frederic G. Renner

Cowpunchers were mighty particular about their rig an' in all the camps you'd find a fashion leader....From a cowpuncher's idea, these fellars was sure good to look at. Of course, a good many of these fancy men were more ornamental than useful... but one of the best cow-hands I ever knew belonged to this class...he's the fanciest cow dog I ever see, an' dont think he dont savy the cow. He knows what she says to her calf.

CMR

John Saylor, Brusett

79

IN TOWN

IN WITHOUT KNOCKING, 1909

oil, 20⅛" × 29⅞"

Courtesy Amon Carter Museum, Fort Worth

Bison Bar, Miles City

82

Jim and Ossia Kearns at a barn dance, Henry Barron Ranch, Townsend

Men's room papered with CMR prints, Oxen Yoke Inn, Utica

84

Annual branding party, Oxen Yoke Inn, Utica

BRONCRIDERS AND BULLDOGGERS

BRONC IN COW CAMP, 1897
oil, 20″ × 31″
Courtesy of Amon Carter Museum, Fort Worth

...I never got to be a bronk rider but in my youthfull days wanted to be and while that want lasted I had a fine chance to study hoss enatimy from under and over   the under was the view a taripan gits   The over while I hoverd ont the end of a Macarty rope was like the eagle sees grand but dam scary for folks without wings...

CMR

Riders from the Cornwell Ranch watching the Ranch Roundup competition, Miles City

Bucking Horse Sale, Miles City

90

Warrick Rodeo, Bear Paw Mountains

Horse rearing out of chute, Bucking Horse Sale, Miles City

92

...I have lived among riders most of my life and late years Iv been taking in contests at different places but yours has got them all skined to the dew claws An Il take my hat off to aney rider who takes or tryes to drag a prize from you   An Injun once told me that bravery came from the hart not the head. If my red brother is right Bronk riders and bull dogers are all hart above the wast band but its a good bet theres nothing under there hat but hair...

CMR

Saddlebronc rider Hank Franzen, Miles City

Reuben Busenitz, Miles City

Charles M. Russell Stampede, Stanford

(Above and opposite) Warrick Rodeo,
near Rocky Boy Indian Reservation,
Bear Paw Mountains

96

Bulldogging, Crow Fair

Wild horse roundup, Standoff

Bareback rider Bill Head, Crow Fair

100

Barrel racer consoled by her husband, Crow Fair

Eastern Montana Fairgrounds, Miles City

Informal barbecue and dance after the rodeo, Miles City

103

RANGE WINTERS

CHRISTMAS AT THE LINE CAMP, 1904
watercolor, 14½″ × 20¾″
Courtesy Amon Carter Museum, Fort Worth

...for three moons the trails have hidden beneath the snow an it is not good to travel far when the poney wares his hair long My arms is short an cannot reach the pipe you light for me but our harts are together and the same   it is good

CMR

Gerald Mack, winterkeeper of the Ken Perry Ranch, Little Belt Mountains

Jake Hoover Cabin, restored by Bill Trask, Little Belt Mountains

Cowboy artist Buckeye Blake, deserted line camp, Missouri Breaks

Fox and beaver pelts on packhorses, Hoover Cabin

Feeding, Ken Perry Ranch, Utica

Feeding wagon pulled by workhorses, Frank Urick Ranch, Belt

Hugo Tureck's truck, Square Butte

WAITING FOR A CHINOOK, 1886

watercolor, 2″ × 4″

Courtesy Montana Stockgrowers Association, Helena

Chief Mountain, Glacier National Park

...I remember one day we were looking at buffalo carcus and you said Russ I wish I was a Sioux Injun a hundred years ago   and I said me to Ted thairs a pair of us

I have often made that wish since an if the buffalo would come back tomorrow I wouldent be slow shedding to a brich clout and youd trade that three duce ranch for a buffalo hoss and a pair ear rings   like many I know, your all Injun under the hide and its a sinch you wouldent get home sick in a skin lodge

Old Ma Nature was kind to her red children and the old time cow puncher was her adopted son...

CMR

Sherman Ranch, Cardston, Alberta

THE OLD WAY

...it pleases me plenty to know that thair is so maney men and wimen that will quit a gas wagon and a good road and ore wilen to look at the world with a horse under em. and where you live Guy if theyl step in the middel of a hoss you can show folks the top of America the wildest the bigest and for a Nature Lover the best part of it...

CMR

Blood Indian horses and approaching blizzard, Canadian Rockies, Standoff

Roundup, Mike Bryant Ranch, Square Butte

Trygue Brown, 4th of July, Bear Paw Mountains

My Brother we are both from the big hills But our fires have been far apart   We met in a strange land   Lonesumniss makes strong friends of shy strangers   In this big camp where the lodges hide the sun and its people rube sholders but do not speek your pipe was mine   It is good our harts are the same

CMR

Moonrise, Standoff

Buffalo, National Bison Range, Moiese